HOWELL

Beginner's guide to

Aquarium Plants & Decoration

Joseph B. Stilton

Editor
Dennis Kelsey-Wood

HOWELL BOOK HOUSE Inc.
230 Park Avenue
New York, N.Y. 10169

Library of Congress Cataloging-in-Publication Data

Stilton, Joseph B.
  Howell beginner's guide to aquarium plants & decoration.

  Summary: Discusses the botany, choice, and growing of suitable plants for the home aquarium and the best forms of decoration for the tank.
  1. Aquarium plants. 2. Aquariums. [1. Aquarium plants. 2. Aquariums] I. Kelsey-Wood, Dennis. II. Title.
III. Title: Beginner's guide to aquarium plants & decoration.
SF457.7.S68   1986   639.3′4   86-3012
ISBN 0-87605-901-9

Book design by Routedale Ltd, Cornwall, England.

Printed in Hong Kong through Bookbuilders Ltd.

Photographics and illustrations:
© Paradise Press
© John Coborn pp 41 and 46 (top)
Line drawings by Peter Daly

Contents

Introduction

In most fishkeeping books designed for the beginner, space does not permit detailed information on the choice and care of aquatic plants or on the subject of aquascaping. Aquarium plants, being living forms, require as much care (and in some cases more) as the fishes or other tank inmates, if they are to be kept in the best of health.

The function of plants in the aquarium is not purely decorative. They assist in the recycling of the waste products from the animal inmates of the tank by taking in carbon dioxide during photosynthesis and emitting oxygen, as well as absorbing organic excretory matter. In addition, they provide shelter for the tank's smaller dwellers and equip some fishes with a site on which to lay their eggs.

The life cycle of aquatic plants can be just as interesting as that of fishes and there is room for further study into all aspects of aquarium botany. New species are frequently appearing on the market and even the amateur can soon contribute to the collective knowledge required by all aquarists in their quest for perfectly balanced aquaculture.

7

A tank containing a community of colorful, healthy fishes swimming across an imaginatively prepared landscape, amongst a miniature jungle of lush vegetation in its various subtle shades of green, is a joy to behold. It is not always easy to maintain such an attractive display and, all too often, one sees aquaria containing withered, sorrowful, algae-infested plants which are no credit to their owner who, usually through ignorance, has not provided his plants with the basic requirements necessary to enable them to flourish. Tanks seen in bars, restaurants, receptions and even some public aquaria often fall into this latter category. The author finds it difficult to understand how the owners can justify having such an unprofessional looking display in what may otherwise be a very efficient establishment. The answer, of course, is that if one is unable, for whatever reason, to maintain his aquaria (particularly those on view to the public) to the highest standards of aquaculture, then there is little constructive purpose in having them at all.

The creation and maintenance of a balanced environment with plants and animals in the aquarium is a science within itself and it is the purpose of this little book to introduce the beginner to the joys of underwater gardening in order that an attractive and fitting home can be created for the plants and fish alike.

A harmonious blend of fish and plants is what all aquarists strive to achieve.

1. Basic Botany

In order to understand the requirements of his plants the aquaculturist, like the gardener, must have at least some basic knowledge of botany. Just as zoology is the study of the members of the animal kingdom, so botany encompasses research into all aspects of the realm of plants — ranging from the simplest microscopic, single-celled forms, to the largest of all life forms, the trees. There are many branches of botany, each of which may assist us in our aquacultural interests. Taxonomy is the study of naming and classifying plants, physiology the examination of the functions of their internal structure and ecology the science of the interaction of plants and animals with their natural environment.

Classification of Plants

With the infinite variety and numbers of different kinds of plants, a system of classification for scientists studying them became essential. In the 18th century, the Swedish botanist Carl Linnaeus pioneered both zoological and botanical classification in a method now known as taxonomy. He devised a binomial system based on the mutual affinities of plants or animals. The plant kingdom is therefore arranged according to common characteristics. Most aquatic plants fall into the classes Monocotyledon (single seed-leaf), Dicotyledon (double seed-leaf), Bryophyta (mosses) or Pteriodophyta (ferns). Within these classes are a number of orders, each containing a number of families, which in turn contain a number of genera. For our purposes and to keep matters simple, we will classify from the family. For example, an aquarium plant commonly known as tape grass would appear as follows:

FAMILY	*Hydrocharitaceae*
GENUS	*Vallisneria*
SPECIES	*spiralis*

In naming the plant, only the generic and specific name is used, *Vallisneria spiralis*, this being the binomial to which we have already referred. There are several species within the genus *Vallisneria* each with similarities to the others, thus: *V. americana*, *V. asiatica* and *V. gigantea*. Whilst discussing species in a particular genus with which we are already familiar one can use just the capital initial of the generic name as we have done here.

9

To the beginner, the scientific naming of plants may, at first, seem over-complicated and pointless when one can apparently use common English names but, with a little application, one will soon learn to use these names with the skill of a qualified botanist and realise the need to recognize the characteristics of plants which may not even have a common name. Conversely, it must be appreciated that a plant (or animal) may have many common names — depending on the regions, as well as countries, in which it is found. This can create considerable confusion which the application of the binomial system of nomenclature — used internationally — overcomes, including language barriers.

Unfortunately, there is no easy way of classifying water plants using official botanical taxonomy as many of the genera contain both aquatic and terrestrial forms. In chapter 3, an alternative method of classifying aquatic plants for aquarists will be discussed.

Simple Plant Physiology

All plants used in the aquarium are chlorophyll-containing green forms which require the energy of sunlight to form organic building substances from carbon dioxide and water. The products of this complicated process, which is known as photosynthesis and occurs in all green parts of the plant, are carbohydrates (sugars and starches), fats and proteins — all essential components of a healthy plant. Further important nutrients, in the form of dissolved mineral salts and organic materials, are obtained in various ways through root systems or by direct absorption through leaves or stems.

The importance of a correct light source for all green plants cannot be underestimated. Being positively phototropic, green stems will grow towards a light source. Green leaves are usually diaphototropic in that they will lay horizontal to the light source in order to obtain maximum illumination, whilst the roots of many water plants are negatively phototropic and will grow away from the light source.

The structure of water plants reflects the adaptation to the environment in which they grow and shows fundamental differences to that of terrestrial forms. In most aquatic species the major part of the stem tissue consists of the aerenchyma (a sponge-like structure with large spaces between the cells, necessary to maintain buoyancy). A bundle of nutrient transporting vessels radiating into the leaves forms the central part of the stem. A single layer of living cells, the endodermis, encases this inner transport system. The roots are also composed chiefly of aerenchyma and, unlike terrestrial plants, there is no root-cap. Root hairs only appear when the plant is firmly anchored in the substrate. The leaves of many water plants are extremely thin and the chloroplasts (chlorophyll bearing cells) are contained only in the epidermis (outer layer). Pores only occur on the upper sides of the leaves of water plants and, in the case of floating leaves, gas exchange takes place in the air only.

Many species of aquatic plants exhibit heterophylly (different shaped leaves,

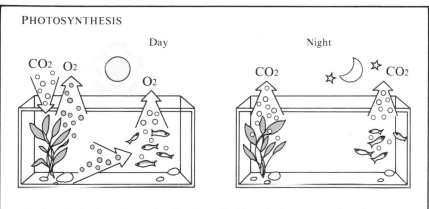

PHOTOSYNTHESIS

Day   Night

CO_2 O_2 CO_2 CO_2
                    O_2

During the daytime, plants absorb carbon dioxide and release oxygen into the water.
At night, no oxygen is manufactured by the plants which release only carbon dioxide.
Plants are thus useful for supplementing the existing supply of this element in the tank.

sometimes with different functions, on the same plant), some even having aquatic, floating and aerial forms.

Aquarium plants come in an amazing diversity of form and biological types but the basic physiological functions are similar in most cases. Perhaps the biggest differences lie in the methods of reproduction. Sexual reproduction includes the formation of egg and sperm cells which fuse together to form spores or seeds depending on the plant type. The process can be complicated and may be difficult to accomplish under aquarium conditions. Luckily, most aquatic plants are also capable of asexual (vegetative) reproduction, which is a method of increasing in numbers without producing seeds or spores and includes runners, stolons, offsets, rhizomes and tubers.

The Ecology of Aquarium Plants

The aim of every serious aquaculturist is to strike a perfect balance between the animals, plants and the environment in his tank. Environmental conditions, which are important to plants and which may vary from species to species, include light intensity, photoperiod (hours of illumination), temperature, water depth, pressure, alkalinity or acidity, gas content, mineral content, humus content and water movement.

Ideally, one should have a good knowledge of the plants' natural habitats, which may vary from fast-flowing, alkaline streams to broad, soft-watered rivers; from murky, muddy swamps to open sunlit lakes. If you know the part of the world from where your plant originates, climatic and topographical information may be gleaned from a good world atlas. Other information is not so easy to obtain unless you are fortunate enough to be able to visit the area in question so you will have to resort to researching books, papers or tapping the knowledge of more experienced aquarists.

2. Aquaculture

Aquaculture can be described as that branch of horticulture which is applied to water plants and is, perhaps, a more appropriate description than underwater gardening. In general, most aquatic plants are easier to grow than some of the more difficult varieties of garden plant, although there will be obvious variations in the conditions required from species to species. Many aquatic plants will survive quite happily in clean, washed aquarium sand, the waste products from the animal inhabitants of the tank providing the necessary nutrients. Artificial, or natural, fertilizers should never be used in the aquarium as it is almost impossible to strike the correct balance. All fertilizers contain nitrates which, in excessive quantities, will constitute a real danger to the fishes. In chapter 3, cultivation tips will be given for each described plant but the following general points will be found useful.

Water Conditions

Some plants (and fishes) come from soft waters, others from hard waters. Soft waters are usually slightly acidic and have a low pH (below 7), whilst hard waters contain varying quantities of mainly calcium based dissolved material salts, and are usually alkaline with a high pH (above 7). The pH scale, which is based on the quantities of hydrogen ions contained in a given substance, indicates degrees of acidity or alkalinity in which 7 is neutral. Values below 7 are acid and the lower the number, the more acid it is.

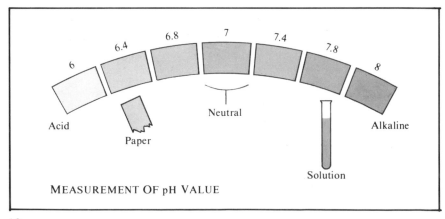

MEASUREMENT OF pH VALUE

Aquarium water should never be below pH 5.5. Values above 7 are alkaline and, in the aquarium, rarely above pH 8.5. Plants which are native to acidic waters will not do well in an aquarium with a pH above 7 and vice versa. Various proprietary pH test kits are available on the market. The best types are those in which a drop of indicator fluid colors a sample of the water contained in a glass tube. The color is then compared against a chart which gives a pH value for each color shade. There are various ways of adjusting the pH in your water. Buffer solutions may be purchased from your supplier and used to the manufacturer's instructions. The presence of peat in your planting medium will help reduce the pH value of the water. Where tap-water is hard and you require soft water for your aquarium, it is best to use rainwater which may be collected in a water butt.

Hardness in water, which is due to the presence of the dissolved salts of mainly calcium and magnesium, can be measured in degrees of hardness (DH). The German measure of 1° DH is equivalent to 10 milligrams of calcium oxide dissolved in 1 litre of water and is the system mainly used by aquarists. In the British or American system, 1 degree of hardness equals 14.3 parts per million (PPM) of calcium carbonate. The two systems can be converted as follows:

$$\text{German degrees (DH)} = \text{British or US degrees} \times \frac{100}{56}$$

$$\text{British or US degrees} = \text{German degrees (DH)} \times \frac{56}{100}$$

For the purposes of this book the German system will be used but, as you can see, there is no problem in converting into British or US. The values can be measured using comparator tests available from your supplier, following the instructions supplied by the manufacturer. The use of a hydrometer will also give you some indication of the amount of dissolved salts in water.

One problem which is often overlooked in the use of hard water is the phenomenon known as chemical prostration. Aquarists are often puzzled by the demise in what were apparently healthy fishes and plants. All of the basic rules may have been adhered to, including the regular topping-up of the tank to replace water lost by evaporation. It is a fundamental fact that, if you evaporate the water from a solution of almost any substance, the chemical content will stay in the remaining water. A good example of this fact is the forming of 'fur' on the inner surface of a kettle in which hard water is frequently boiled. The deposit consists of mainly calcium salts which have gradually built up each time the kettle is boiled. A similar process will occur in the aquarium albeit at a much slower rate. In aquaria topped up with hard water over a long period, the hardness of the water will increase to such an extent that it will be a danger to all life in the tank; even to those fishes and plants which would normally tolerate an average degree of hardness.

Normal filtration of the water will only remove suspended matter and not chemicals in solution so the problem must be tackled from the beginning. Once you have achieved the correct hardness in your water for the community which you are keeping, all topping up must be done with, preferably, distilled water but unpolluted rainwater makes a good substitute. Distilled water can usually be purchased quite cheaply from a local manufacturer or drug store. If it is not possible to obtain distilled water or sufficient rainwater at a particular time, and you are worried about the excessive degree of hardness in your water, then you can carefully remove up to 75% of the tank's water content and replace it with tap water which has been left standing for 48 hours (to allow any chlorine content to disperse). Needless to say, temperature synchronization is important when you are doing this as you will not want to risk the possibility of thermal shock to your fishes or plants.

Another important factor in water conditions for plants is the presence of adequate air and carbon dioxide. During the daylight hours plants absorb dissolved carbon dioxide from the water in the process of photosynthesis. Recent research has shown that, where the fish content of the tank is inadequate, there may be an insufficient supply of carbon dioxide for the plants. It is now possible to obtain small cylinders of carbon dioxide so that a supplementary supply of the gas can be added to the water.

One fact often overlooked is that plants also respire and, while they may have to dispel surplus oxygen during the day, they need to absorb it from the air content of the water at nightime.

Planting Media

Although many plants will grow, after a fashion, in washed aquarium gravel or sand, if you require fast, lush-green growth from rooted stock it is adviseable to have a layer of loam and/or peat under the top, 'decorative' layer. The ideal medium for most aquarium plants is as follows: place a 1cm (½ in) layer of unwashed river sand on the aquarium bottom and cover this with a mosaic of peat slabs (which have been weighted down and thoroughly soaked for at least two weeks about 1-2½cm (½-1in) thick. Spaces of about 1cm (½ in) left between the peat slices can be filled with garden loam which has been sterilized by baking it in a hot oven for about 15 minutes. This is then covered with a further layer of unwashed river sand about 1cm (½ in) thick and the whole is finally covered with washed river sand or aquarium gravel which should effectively weigh down the other ingredients and prevent lighter particles from floating to the surface when the water is added.

As the aquarium substrate is normally sloped upwards from the front of the tank to the rear it is this final layer of gravel which should be 2-3cm (1 - 1½ in) deep in the foreground, sloping up to 5-7cm (2 - 3 in) depth at the back. For any further terracing work, using rocks as retainers, washed gravel only should be used, the layer of peat and loam in the lower layers being adequate for lush plant growth.

River sand or gravel can be obtained from the beds of fast flowing streams and can be graded by sieving; alternatively, ready graded aquarium gravel can be obtained from your aquarists' supplier but, whatever the source, it should be thoroughly washed before you use it as a top layer for your aquarium substrate. Place the gravel in a large metal container and pour on quantities of boiling water until it is covered and leave for about 30 minutes. This will kill off any potentially dangerous bugs which may be present in the medium. Next, pass a rubber pipe, which is attached at one end to your cold water tap, into the bucket of sand and swirl it about near the bottom, allowing the excess water and floating dirt to overflow into the drain. This process should continue until the water remains crystal clear even when the surface of the gravel is swirled about.

Planting

Before you plant out your aquarium tank it is a good idea to sketch out a few ideas on paper on how you want your final layout to look, remembering to leave plenty of open swimming space for the fish. The usual pattern is to have a plant-free swimming area, slightly off centre of the foreground. Plants may be loosely divided into foreground, middleground and background types, depending on their growing height. We will look at the various layout possibilities in Chapter 4.

Diagrams 1-4 illustrate progressive improvement of tank layout.

Having prepared your substrate, a small amount of water to about 2cm (1 in) above the surface of the gravel should be added, taking care not to disturb the lower layers. Check your plants carefully, removing any dead or decaying leaves. Initially, the plants should be weighted to prevent them floating to the surface when the ltank is filled with water. The author does not recommend the use of any metallic weighting materials which may pollute the water. Glass or ceramic beads, tied loosely near the plants' roots with nylon thread, are ideal. Using a special forked planting tool the roots and the beads are pushed gently into the surface gravel until they are covered, again taking care not to disturb the lower layers. The roots of the plants will soon grow into the peat and loam layer and form a dense mat.

15

After all the planting has been carried out the tank can be carefully filled with water. This should be done very slowly and, preferably, the water poured via a flat dish resting on the substrate to prevent concentrated disturbance in any particular area. After planting, be patient and leave the tank for a few days before adding the fish; in fact two weeks to allow the plants to completely settle and to get a good root footing will not go amiss. It obviously defeats the object if you spend a great deal of time planting your tank, allowing the plants to settle and then add a group of boisterous, plant-eating fishes, or those which enjoy rooting up the substrate in search of food. Goldfish are amongst the worst plant-eaters, whilst some of the larger barbs and cichlids seem to get great enjoyment from uprooting your valuable plants. If you intend to keep such vandals you must use extremely robust plants and allow them to develop a thorough root system before adding the fish, use artificial plants or dispense with plants altogether. Some smaller browsing fishes such as mollies, will take the occasional nibble at the leaves but they seem to do little harm; in fact they may do some good by removing algae. Snails can be harmful to aquarium plants and, in particular, the Colombian Ramshorn and the Japanese live-bearing snails can soon reduce them to mere skeletons. If you want to have snails, and a good balance in your tank, you will have to carry out frequent snail culling operations.

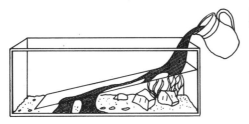

METHOD OF POURING
WATER INTO TANK

Plant Maintenance

Plants should be regularly serviced, dead and dying leaves should be pinched out and removed completely from the tank. If you require more bushy growth, the growing tips can be pinched out and this will encourage the side shoots to flourish.

Lighting is of utmost importance to tropical water plants and you require the tank to be well illuminated for at least twelve hours each day. Artificial lighting, controlled by a time switch, appears to be the most efficient way of maintaining a constant light/dark cycle. Correct light intensity is also important; too strong a light will encourage excessive algal growth, not only on the rocks and glass but also on the plants themselves. The use of masking tape on the light tubes will reduce light intensity, as will the planting of one or two surface growing plants. There are no hard and fast rules and the correct balance will only be found after a certain amount of trial and error. Some catfish such as the *Plecostomus* will help remove algae from the plant leaves without causing damage to the plants themselves.

3. Choice of Plants

There are many hundreds of different species of aquatic plants which can be grown in the aquarium and new species are constantly being brought to the attention of the aquarist. It would be impossible to describe more than a few species in a book of this size, so the author has chosen to select a number of plants which represent a cross section of the different types. Most of those described are inexpensive, easy to grow and serve the purposes of decoration, oxygenation and recycling of waste materials as well as providing hiding places and spawning sites for the fishes. For the benefit of the beginner with wider ambition, one or two 'difficult' varieties have been added to whet his appetite.

Plants are usually obtained from a dealer, from a fellow aquarist who has a surplus or, if you are fortunate enough to live in an area where given plants grow in the wild, you can collect your own. In certain areas the propagation of aquatic plants is fairly big business and countries such as Singapore, which have favorable climates, export aquatic plants to other parts of the world in great numbers. When purchasing plants, only select stock which appears healthy and has good signs of vigorous growth. Signs of decay on the leaves, stems or rootstock should be avoided.

For convenience to the beginner, it is desirable to classify the plants into types depending on their method of growth as follows:

Type 1. Small floating plants, with or without short roots.

Type 2. Larger floating plants with root systems which grow well into the water and may, or may not, anchor into the substrate.

Type 3. Plants which root into the substrate and stay wholly underwater (with the exception of the flowers in some species).

Type 4. Plants with leaves partly above and partly below the water surface. They invariably flower above water.

Type 5. Plants which root into the substrate and have leaves and flowers which float horizontally on the water surface.

Type 6. Marsh plants in which the root stock is submerged, the remainder of the plant being above the water surface.

In the following descriptions, an indication of the type will be given, along with brief notes on distribution, cultivation and the types of plants which will mix well in a community tank. For ease of reference the plants are arranged in alphabetic order and a glossary of terminology is included at the end of the book.

Acorus gramineus   Sweet Flag   Type 3/4

General: Although typically a marsh plant, this species can be grown completely underwater in the aquarium. Leaves are stiff and grass-like and grow to 60cm (24 in) in length. One variety has attractive variegated leaves.

Distribution: North-east Asia. (China, Japan).

Cultivation: Prefers strong light and humus in the substrate. Water conditions neutral to slightly acid (pH 7.0 - 6.5) and water hardness DH 10-20. Cannot tolerate high temperatures for long periods and is best suited to temperate aquaria (18-22°C). For propagation the rootstock can be divided.

Community: May be kept together with *Cryptocoryne, Vallisneria, Ceratopteris.*

Anubias lanceolata   Type 4

General: A marsh plant with dark green lanceolate leaves which are partly submerged and grow to about 20cm (8 in) long. The flower consists of a spadix enveloped within a green spathe.

Distribution: Central West Africa.

Cultivation: Best cultivated as a marsh plant in soft water. A sandy substrate containing loam is required and a temperature around 25°C will suit. It may be propagated by rootstock division.

Community: Grows well with *Aponogeton, Vallisneria, Ceratopteris.*

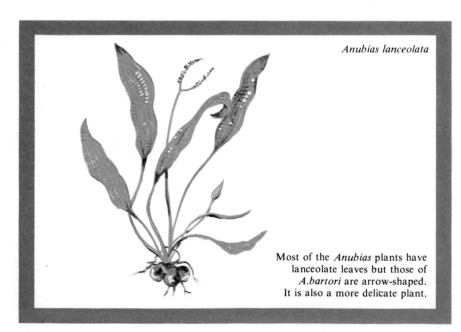

Anubias lanceolata

Most of the *Anubias* plants have lanceolate leaves but those of *A.bartori* are arrow-shaped. It is also a more delicate plant.

There are about forty-five species in this genus and the most popular are *crispus, undulatus, ulvaceous* and the delicate *fenestralis*.

Aponogeton
bernerianus

Aponogeton bernerianus   Type 4

General: Like all *Aponogeton* species it has a tuberous rootstock, in this case some 2-3cm (1 in) in diameter. The long, dark green leaves are heavily veined in a lattice-like pattern which results in squarish 'windows' where the leaf mesophyll has fallen out. Flowers, on pairs of small spikes, are pinkish in color.

Distribution: The island of Madagascar.

Cultivation: Plant the tubers in early spring in small flower-pots containing a mixture of equal parts of unwashed sand, charcoal and clay. Immerse in soft, shallow water (DH 3-5) which is slightly acidic to neutral (pH 6.5 - 7.0), at a temperature of 23-26°C. Allow the shoots to sprout well before transferring to the aquarium where they are best retained in their pots. Most *Aponogeton* species hibernate in the winter so potted plants can easily be moved into colder water (15 - 18°C) for 2 or 3 months.

Community: Will tolerate other species of *Aponogeton* and *Ceratopteris*.

19

Aponogeton crispus   Type 4

General: This species has a tuberous rootstock 2-4cm (1 - 1½ in) in diameter.
The leaves have wavy margins, are light green in color and grow to
about 30cm (12 in) in length.
Distribution: Sri Lanka (Ceylon).
Cultivation: One of the easier species in the genus; will tolerate a range of
water conditions and is thus widely popular with aquarists. The
rootstock can be planted directly into the aquarium substrate.
Keep at a temperature of about 22°C.
Community: Can be planted with some *Cryptocoryne* species, other species of
Aponogeton, Ceratopteris and *Acorus.*

Aponogeton elongatus   Type 4

General: Leaves are similar in appearance to those of *A. crispus* but narrower,
growing to about 25cm (10 in).
Distribution: Northern and Eastern Australia.
Cultivation: Another popular aquarium plant which will grow in water with a
pH of 6.5 - 7.5. Prefers medium light intensity.
Community: Will grow well together with *Vallisneria, Ceratophyllum* and
Myriophyllum.
Other species of *Aponogeton* popular with aquarists include
A. madagascariensis, A. natans, A. ulvaceus and *A. undulatus.*

Bacopa amplexicaulis   Giant Bacopa   Type 4

General: Bacopa is a marsh plant which also does well in the aquarium. The
erect stem grows to 60cm (24 in) in length and the small oval leaves
are opposed. The small blue flowers appear above the water
surface.
Distribution: Southern and Central USA.
Cultivation: Will tolerate the usual sand, peat, loam substrate well. It should
be planted in bunches of several stems together. Water hardness
should not exceed 10 DH and a temperature of 20°C is adequate. It
is easy to propagate from cuttings.
Community: Tolerates *Sagittaria, Ludwigia, Elodea* and *Myriophyllum.*

Bacopa monniera   Type 3/4

General: Smaller than the preceeding species, this is perhaps more suited to the
aquarium. The leaves are slightly darker in color.
Distribution: The old world tropics, Australia, southern Europe, southern
USA.
Cultivation: Will tolerate a wide range of temperatures from 15-25°C.
Requires soft to medium-hard water and prefers a coarse substrate
and strong light.
Community: *Sagittaria, Ludwigia, Myriophyllum.*

20

The Giant Bacopa is suitable for large, deep tanks .....

... but there are smaller species available for most tank sizes as seen in the display below.

The elegant Hornwort is a first
class oxygenating plant.

Barclaya longifolia   Type 5

General: This beautiful plant has long, arrow-shaped, leaves of green with a
  reddish tinge. After growing from the rootstock, the leaves
  eventually float horizontally on the water surface. The flowers are
  about 2½cm (1 in) in diameter and purplish in color.
Distribution: South-east Asia.
Cultivation: Not an easy species to cultivate but well worth the effort.
  Substrate should contain charcoal and clay. Perhaps best grown in
  pots. Water should be soft with a pH of 6.0 - 7.0, DH 4-8.
  Temperature should never drop below 25°C and bottom heat is
  recommended. (Heating cable in the substrate).
Community: Best kept with plants which require similar conditions such as
  Cryptocoryne and *Ceratopteris.*

Cabomba aquatica   Type 3

General: A very decorative aquarium plant with stems which can reach 200cm
  (78 in) in length — given the water depth. The dark green opposed
  leaves are divided into fine feathery segments. The yellow flowers
  bloom above the water surface and are accompanied with small
  circular floating leaves.
Distribution: Tropical South America.
Cultivation: This is a sensitive plant which requires peat and clay in the
  substrate. Water should be soft with a pH of 6.5 - 7.0 and DH
  under 6. Temperature should not drop below 18°C and should
  average 24°C. This plant requires good lighting and responds well
  to broad-spectrum fluorescent tubes. It may be propagated by top
  cuttings.
Community: Not very tolerant towards other plants and best grown on its
  own.

Ceratophyllum demersum   Hornwort   Type 3

General: This species and the closely related *C. submersum* are popular with
  cold-water aquarists. The leaves are feathery and very delicate.
  Stalks may grow to 150cm (60 in) in length but aquarium depth
  regulates growth. A totally submersed plant which flowers below
  the water surface.
Distribution: Cosmopolitan.
Cultivation: Prefers a fairly dense substrate with clay. Water should be hard
  with a pH value of 8.0 - 8.5 and a DH of 15-30. This plant does best
  at temperatures below 18°C.
Community: Best kept with plants which will tolerate lower temperatures such
  as *Vallisneria.*

Cabomba aquatica, one of the many species in this genus. Another popular variety is *C.caroliniana*.

Ceratopteris thalictroides   **Water Sprite**   **Type 2 and 3**

General: This aquatic fern comes in two forms one of which floats freely on the water surface, the other roots into the substrate. The fine fern-like leaves are brittle and grow to about 70cm (28 in) in length.

Distribution: Found throughout the tropics.

Cultivation: This popular aquarium plant is fast growing given the correct conditions including acid water of pH 5.5 - 6.5 and DH well under 10. Peat and loam in the substrate is a necessity as is strong light. Propagation is easy from offsets. Temperature best in the region of 25°C.

Community: Suitable for growing with *Acorus, Cabomba, Cryptocoryne, Limnophila* and *Ludwigia*.

Cryptocoryne affinis   **Type 4**

General: The genus *Cryptocoryne* contains a large number of species suitable as aquarium plants. *C. affinis* has leaves which are dark green on the upper surface and wine red beneath. They grow to about 15cm (6 in) in length. The flower consists of a spadix and a spathe.

24

Distribution: Tropical South-east Asia.
Cultivation: Will grow in a medium containing peat and loam. Water should be soft, about 5 DH, with a pH value of 6.0 - 7.0. *C. affinis* is probably the hardiest of the genus and will tolerate a temperature as low as 18°C but is happier at an average of 24°C. A heated substrate is also beneficial for all *Cryptocoryne* species and they require a medium light source. This species may be propagated by plantlets which emerge from root runners.
Community: Other *Cryptocoryne* species, *Acorus, Ceratopteris, Hygrophila* and *Limnophila.*

Cryptocoryne balansae   Type 4

General: One of the larger *Cryptocoryne* species the wavy, light green leaves of which will grow to a length of 40cm (16 in). The flower is a spathe some 10cm (4 in) long with a purplish tinge.
Distribution: Indo-China.
Cultivation: Similar to *C. affinis,* but requires deeper water. Strong light will result in the leaves taking on a purplish tinge. Propagation by lateral shoots.
Community: Other *Cryptocoryne* species, *Acorus, Microsorium.*

Several *Cryptocoryne* species show dark coloring which contrasts nicely with the accompanying green plants.

Cryptocoryne nevillii   Type 4

General: This is one of the shorter species, very suitable for foreground planting as it rarely grows longer than 7.5cm (3 in). It spreads very quickly via lateral shoots and, given the correct treatment, will form an attractive grove.

Distribution: Sri Lanka (Ceylon).

Cultivation: Plant in a substrate containing peat and loam. It takes some time to settle but is hardy once it is established. Will tolerate a pH range of 6.5 - 8.0 and a DH of 8, with a temperature around 24°C.

Community: Can be used for foreground planting in tanks with water around neutral.

Cryptocoryne wendtii   Type 4

General: A medium sized species with broad green leaves 15cm (6 in) in length. Provides a nice contrast to some of the narrower leaved varieties.

Distribution: South-east Asia.

Cultivation: Prefers a neutral pH (7.0) and a temperature of around 24°C. Suitable for mid-ground planting in a substrate containing peat and loam. Requires fairly strong light.

Community: Will tolerate other *Cryptocoryne* species, *Acorus, Hygrophila, Limnophila.*

The ever popular Amazon Sword is seen in many tropical aquaria in its numerous forms.

Water Sprite is also known as Indian Fern and is seen in three
leaf varieties these being either broad (as in photo), narrow or
intermediate.

Echinodorus amazonicus   Amazon Sword   Type 4

General: The genus *Echinodorus* contains several species suitable for the
aquarium many of which are commonly named 'Amazon Swords'.
E. amazonicus (formerly *E. brevipedicellatus*) is one of the more
popular and easy to grow varieties. The green, strap-like leaves
grow to about 50cm (20 in) in length. They flower above water on
stems which can reach 100cm (39 in) in length and the small blooms
are white in color.

Distribution: Brazil.

Cultivation: Best grown in a medium of coarse unwashed river sand with
about 10% loam. They may be fed by inserting small, dried out
balls of clay mixed with river mud into the substrate near the roots.
The water should be soft to medium-hard and the temperature
20-25°C. Light may be medium to strong and natural sunlight is
beneficial. Propagation is by runners and plantlets.

Community: Will tolerate other *Echinodorus* species, *Myriophyllum* and
Vallisneria.

Amazon Sword *(Echinodorus tunicatus)*

Echinodorus bleheri   **Amazon Sword**   **Type 4**

General: Formerly known as *E. paniculatus*, this Amazon Sword is similar to the preceeding species and the two are often confused. The green leaves grow to 70cm (28 in) long and the flower stems up to 2m (78 in) above water level.

Distribution: Tropical South America.

Cultivation: Plant into a medium containing peat and loam. Water should be around neutral (pH 7.0) with a medium hardness. Temperature should not drop below 20°C in the winter, with a summer temperature around 26°C. Well established plants may be propagated by rootstock division.

Community: Other *Echinodorus* species, *Myriophyllum* and Vallisneria.

Echinodorus cordifolius   **Type 4**

General: This species has green, heart-shaped leaves which grow to a height of about 25cm (10 in). The rootstock is tuberous and the flower stalk grows up to 1m (39 in) above the water surface.

Distribution: Southern USA, Mexico.

Cultivation: Will grow in the usual type of substrate described for other species in the genus. Long shoots should be regularly trimmed off so that attractive underwater growth is maintained. Water with a pH of 6.5 - 7.5 is suitable and hardness up to 12 DH is tolerated. A temperature of 20-25°C and a medium light source are necessary.

Community: Other *Echinodorus* species, *Elodea, Sagittaria, Vallisneria.*

28

Echnidorus latifolius   Dwarf Amazon Sword   Type 4

General: This species was formerly known as *E. magdalenensis.* It is one of the
easiest in the genus to keep and propagate. The submersed leaves
are long, narrow and sword shaped. Emersed leaves are shorter
and lanceolate.
Distribution: Colombia.
Cultivation: Probably grows best in a substrate with loam and clay. Lighting
medium to strong with a water hardness of no more than 10 DH.
Propagation by runners.
Community: Grows well with other *Echinodorus* species and *Myriophyllum.*

Eichornia crassipes   Water Hyacinth   Type 2

General: This robust floating plant has been included here due to the
decorative qualities of the roots which form dense bunches in
brown, blue and black. The leaves form a rosette and the petioles
are much thickened to form spongy, floating globular structures.
The attractive flowers are purple and white.
Distribution: Tropical South America, Central America and southern USA.
Cultivation: Requires an aquarium with ample top space or may be grown in
greenhouse pools. Strong light is required, as is soft water and a
nutritious substrate.
Community: Best kept on its own where it is useful with destructive fishes
which normally uproot substrate growing plants.

Amazon Sword plants and Discus are a natural combination.

29

Eleocharis acicularis   Hair Grass   Type 3

General: A popular, bright green, grass-like plant, useful for the aquarium foreground. The leaves grow to about 15cm (6 in) and the trailing rootstock sends up many shoots.
Distribution: Cosmopolitan.
Cultivation: Not difficult to grow in an unwashed sand substrate. The water should be acid to neutral and the temperature around 22°C. Propagation is by removing plantlets from the root runners.
Community: Goes well with *Cryptocoryne* species and *Vallisneria*.

Elodea densa   Type 3

General: One of the most popular of all aquarium plants and very suitable for the beginner as it grows quickly and is very tolerant to temperature changes. The stems can grow up to 3m (10 ft) in length but are regulated by water depth. The narrow, light green leaves are 2-3cm (1 in) long and grow in whorls. The small, yellowish flowers grow on a stalk above the water surface.
Distribution: South and Central America.

Hair Grass (also known as Spike Bush) is best seen where it is given an area free of other plants. There are many species native to both the USA and Europe.

Elodea densa is a good oxygenator for tanks.

Cultivation: Will grow well in aquarium gravel without peat. Water conditions should be alkaline with a pH of 7.5 - 9.5 and a hardness of 10-20 DH. Light should be fairly strong and the temperature anywhere between 15 and 25°C. Propagation is by cuttings simply inserted into the substrate.

Community: Will grow with other alkali tolerant plants such as *Myriophyllum* and *Sagittaria.* The closely ralted *Elodea canadensis,* (Canadian Pond Weed) is very suitable for cold-water aquaria.

Hydrocotyle vulgaris   Water Pennywort   Type 3/5

General: This plant is popular due to its unusually round shaped leaves which are normally surface floaters but the form *H. vulgaris* submersa is suitable for the aquarium. The leaves are 2-4cm (1-1½ in) in diameter on a stalk about 10cm (4 in) long.

Distribution: Europe and North Africa.

Cultivation: A substrate containing peat and clay is suitable for this plant which likes a fairly neutral water (pH 6.5 - 7.5). It will tolerate temperatures in the range 18-25°C. Propagation is by cuttings from the creeping rootstock.

Community: This plant will grow well with *Microsorium* and *Elodea.*

31

Hygrophila difformis   Water Wisteria   Type 3

General: Formerly known as *Synnema triflorum,* this is a very popular plant amongst aquarists. It bears a similarity to *Ceratopteris* but its leaves are larger and denser. It grows to about 12cm (5 in) in length.
Distribution: South-east Asia.
Cultivation: Requires peat and clay in the substrate and will benefit with the addition of a little charcoal. Water should be slightly acid to neutral (ph 6.0 - 7.0) and soft — around 10 DH. It grows best in a temperature of 25-28°C. Propagation is easy from cuttings as well as rootstock division.
Community: *Cryptocoryne, Lymnophila* and *Ceratopteris.*

Isoetes malinverniana   Type 3

General: This unusual aquatic fern, forms rosettes of thin, threadlike leaves which grow to the water surface and float like ribbons.
Distribution: Southern Europe.
Cultivation: This decorative plant requires an acid water (pH 5.0 - 6.5). A sandy substrate with peat and clay is necessary and a temperature not exceeding 22°C. It does not require too strong a light. Propagation is by spores which will germinate on damp peat.
Community: *Vallisneria* and *Lobelia.*

Lemna minor   Duckweed   Type 1

General: This small, common floating plant consists of pairs of light green circular leaves 2 - 3mm in diameter. Rootlets up to 1cm (½ in) in length grow into the water from the centre of the underside. It rarely flowers, but quickly reproduces vegetatively. It is useful as food for plant-eating fishes and will often reproduce so vigorously that large quantities must be removed from the water surface before it cuts out too much light from the other plants.
Distribution: Cosmopolitan.
Cultivation: No special requirements; it will grow in most water conditions and temperatures.
Community: Must be kept well under control if in community with other plants.

Limnobium stoloniferum   Type 1

General: This floating plant has rosettes of green, circular leaves each about 2 - 3cm (1 in) in diameter. The long bundles of roots are attractive and provide good hiding places for fry.
Distribution: Central and South America.
Cultivation: Requires strong light at the surface as well as high humidity so it is best to cover the tank with a sheet of glass. Water should be soft to medium hard with a pH around 7.0. Temperature 20 - 25°C..
Community: Suitable for tanks with *Cabomba* and *Myriophyllum.*

Hydrocotyle vulgaris (Pennywort)

Water
Wisteria

Ambulia provides good hiding places for these Barbs and Tetras.

Limnophila indica   **Ambulia**   Type 3

General: An aquatic plant with fine feathery leaves *L. indica* and the closely related *L. heterophylla* make attractive additions to the aquarium. The leaves are in whorls on stems which grow to 50cm (20 in) in length. It is said that the sap of these plants is toxic to fishes when freshly cut so cuttings should be rooted before adding to the tank.

Distribution: Africa, South-east Asia, Australia.

Cultivation: Not a very demanding plant but prefers strong light, a temperature of 20-25°C. and a pH of 6.5 - 7.0. Propagation is by cuttings or seeds.

Community: Associates well with *Acorus, Cryptocoryne* and *Vallisneria.*

Lobelia cardinalis   Type 3

General: The submersed form of this plant is suitable for the aquarium. The thick stems grow to 30cm (12 in) and the dark green leaves are alternate. The flower stem bears red, bell-shaped flowers.

Distribution: North America.

Cultivation: Suitable for the cold water tank at temperatures not exceeding 20°C. Substrate should contain loam and the pH around neutral (7.0).

Community: *Ludwigia* and *Vallisneria* are suitable community plants with this species.

Ludwigia natans   Type 4

General: An attractive plant in which the underside of the leaves is a deep wine red when sufficient iron is contained in the substrate. The stem is thick and the leaves 2½-5cm (1 - 2 in) long.

Distribution: USA, Mexico.

Cultivation: This fast growing plant makes no special demands on water conditions but requires a temperature of 20-28°C and good light. About 10% loam in the substrate is beneficial.

Community: Makes a good partner for *Lobelia*.

Microsorium pteropus   Java Fern   Type 3

General: This attractive fern may be aquatic or terrestrial in its native habitat. May be grown underwater in the aquarium. The green lanceolate leaves are 10-30cm (4 - 12 in) and grow from a green rhizome.

Distribution: South-east Asia.

Cultivation: This fern should not be planted into the substrate but inserted into cracks in the rocks or attached to roots or driftwood with a fine thread where it will soon anchor itself. Water should be slightly acid to neutral (pH 5.5 - 7.0) and not too hard (6-8 DH). The temperature can be around 25°C. Propagation is by root stock cuttings or from leaf-buds which appear from time to time.

Community: Can be kept with *Cryptocoryne* species, *Acorus* and *Limnophila*.

Java Fern is a popular plant with aquarists as it is attractive and hardy.

Myriophyllum brasiliense Parrot's Feather Type 3

General: Of the 40 or so species of *Myriophyllum* (Water Milfoils), used in the aquarium, *M. brasiliense* is probably the most popular. The long feathery fronds may grow to 150cm (60 in) in length. White flowers may appear on emergent leaves.

Distribution: South America.

Cultivation: Prefers deeper water which is fairly alkaline (pH 7.7 - 10.0) and a hardness up to 16 DH. Requires mud or loam in the substrate but peat should be avoided. A temperature of 20-25°C is suitable.

Community: May be grown with other alkaline loving plants such as *Echinodorus* and *Sagittaria.*

Najas kingii Type 3

General: This delicate water plant has small sickle shaped leaves on a stem which grows to 30cm (12 in) long.

Distribution: South-east Asia.

Cultivation: It requires soft water and a strong light. It does best at temperatures around 25°C.

Community: *Ceratophyllum* and *Myriophyllum.*

Nomaphila stricta Type 4

General: A perennial water plant which has a stem up to 150cm (60 in) long and large, lanceolate leaves up to 15cm (6 in) long. The small, bright blue flowers bloom above the water surface.

Distribution: South-east Asia.

Cultivation: This plant does not require a great deal of substrate nutrients and seems to do better without them. Prefers slightly acid water (pH 6.5) and a temperature around 23°C. Propagation is by cuttings.

Community: Grows well with *Acorus, Ceratopteris, Cryptocoryne* and *Hygrophylla.*

Nymphaea daubenyana Type 5

General: This small water lily is suitable for the shallow aquarium. The floating, circular leaves may reach 20cm (7½ in) in diameter and thus take light away from plants on the aquarium bottom. The flowers are greenish on the outside and blue inside.

Distribution: This is a horticultural hybrid between *N. micrantha* and *N. coerulia.*

Cultivation: Best grown in a pot containing humus and loam topped with coarse sand. Water should be soft and the temperature around 25°C.

Community: Due to its strong demands on the available light, this species is best kept on its own.

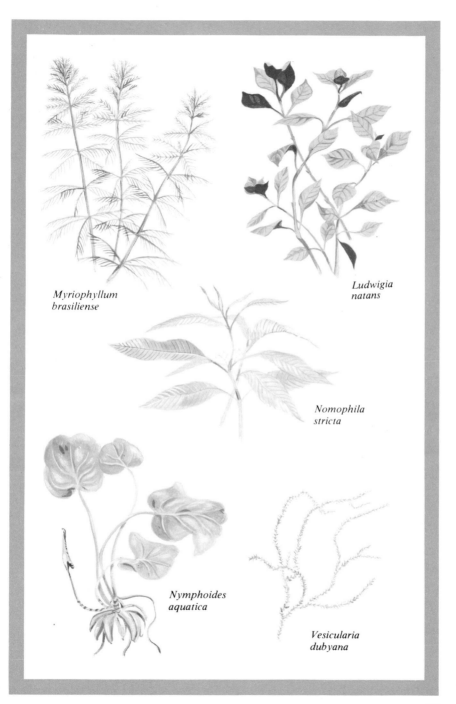

Myriophyllum brasiliense

Ludwigia natans

Nomophila stricta

Nymphoides aquatica

Vesicularia dubyana

37

Nymphoides aquatica   Banana Plant   Type 3/4

General: This plant gets its common name from the banana-shaped root tubers. The leaves are heart-shaped and dark green, sometimes with a reddish tinge. There is a floating leaf stage and it flowers above the water surface.
Distribution: Eastern USA.
Cultivation: Requires bright light and slightly acid water (pH 6.0 - 7.0). Temperature 15-22°C. Substrate should contain a little mud or loam.
Community: *Salvinia* is a good accompanying species.

Pistia stratiotes   Water Lettuce   Type 2

General: Superficially resembling a floating lettuce, this species is an unusual addition to the aquarium. The long feathery roots hang down into the water in bunches and provide an attractive shelter for small fishes.
Distribution: Cosmopolitan (tropical).
Cultivation: Requires a bright light and a high humidity above the water surface. Prefers soft water at a pH of 6.5 - 7.0 and a temperature of 22-25°C. (also above the water surface). It propagates easily from side shoots.
Community: *Cryptocoryne, Hydrocotyle* and other floating plants.

Riccia fluitans   Type 1

General: This small, floating, aquatic liverwort spreads rapidly on the aquarium surface and must be thinned out at regular intervals. It is useful in breeding tanks for foam nest builders.
Distribution: Fairly cosmopolitan.
Cultivation: Requires soft water with a pH of about 6.5. Does best under strong light and a temperature of about 26°C. Easily propagated by division.
Community: *Cryptocoryne* and *Vallisneria.*

Sagittaria platyphylla   Type 4

General: One of several species in the genus, *S. platyphylla* has strap like leaves some 25cm (10 in) long and 2½cm (1 in) wide. Unlike other *Sagittaria species*, the leaves are never arrow-shaped.
Distribution: USA (Valley of the Mississippi).
Cultivation: Use aquarium gravel mixed with about 10% loam and clay in the substrate. Requires strong light and a temperature of 20-25°C. Water should be alkaline with a pH of 8.0 - 10.0.
Community: Other *Sagittaria* species, *Bacopa, Myriophyllum.*

There is a considerable range of leaf shape within the *Sagittaris* genus — here the slender variety *graminea* is seen displayed to good effect.

Salvinia auriculata   Type 1

General: A small floating fern with green, oval leaves about 1.5 - 2.5cm (½ - 1 in) long.

Distribution: Tropical South America.

Cultivation: It requires a strong light and water around neutral (pH 7.0). The temperature should be between 20 and 25°C. Humidity above the water surface is important but it does not tolerate condensation from the tank cover dripping upon it. It is best to dispense with a cover and rely on an aerator to maintain the humidity. Propagates rapidly by lateral shoots.

Community: If it is thinned out at intervals to prevent it shading the light, plants like *Echinodorus* and *Sagittaria* may be grown with it.

Vallisneria spiralis   Tape Grass   Type 3

General: Probably the most popular of all aquarium plants *V. spiralis* consists of a number of tape like leaves up to 60cm (24 in) long and 5-12mm (¼-½ in) wide. The female flowers grow on spiral stems which reach the water surface whilst the male flowers form at the leaf base and float to the surface when ripe.

Distribution: Europe, North America.

Cultivation: This, together with a number of horticultural forms, is an ideal aquarium plant as it will adapt to a wide variety of conditions. It does best in a deep tank with acid water and a strong light.

Community: Will accompany *Aponogeton, Cabomba, Ceratopteris, Cryptocoryne, Elodea, Ludwigia, Myriophyllum* and others.

Vallisnaria spiralis, in its many forms, is often confused with *Sagittaria* species.

A very large tank is needed to create an effect like this.

Vesicularia dubyana   Java Moss   Type 3/4

General: This tropical moss consists of irregularly branched stems with double rows of tiny leaves forming thick tufts. Ideal for small aquaria, especially for some breeding fishes.

Distribution: South-east Asia.

Cultivation: This stalkless plant will attach itself to stones, roots and other aquarium plants. It will tolerate most water conditions and even poor light but does best in mildly acid to neutral soft water (pH 6.0 - 7.0). It appreciates some peat in the substrate and a temperature of 20-25°C.

Community: Will grow in community with *Acorus, Ceratopteris, Cryptocoryne,* and *Vallisneria.*

Veronica beccabunga   European Brooklime   Type 3

General: This species is suitable for cold-water tanks. Stems are approximately 40cm (16 in) long and the opposed green leaves 3-4cm (1 - 1½ in) long.

Distribution: Europe, Asia, North Africa.

Cultivation: Prefers hard alkaline water, rich in oxygen and with some turbulence (from the aerator). Temperatures should be kept below 20°C for most of the time although higher temperatures will occasionally be tolerated.

Community: May be kept with other cold water plants which prefer alkaline to neutral conditions.

41

Plants, fish and rocks in harmony create the aquascene.

4. Aquascaping

Aquascaping is the art of creating a natural looking, underwater landscape within the limits of the available space. As only a small area is available in most aquaria, a certain amount of practice and skill is required to produce a feeling of depth and perspective.

Before setting up a tank it should preferably be placed in its final position to avoid having to move it when the heavy contents have been added and risk breaking the joints. Test for leaks first by filling with water and leaving for a few hours. Any cracks or breaks in the seal can be repaired using silicon rubber compound.

The choice of substrate materials has already been discussed and, of course, will depend on the types of plants to be kept. However, coarse sand or gravel should always be used for the upper layer to prevent the other materials, such as mud, clay, loam or peat, being stirred up by the fishes and clouding the water. Normally, the substrate will slope upwards from the front to the back of the tank and, if the upper edge of the gravel is arranged below the edge of the front frame, it will look more attractive than being able to see below gravel. With frameless tanks it is possible to make an artificial frame from decorative, adhesive tape.

Equipment

Various mechanical equipment is used in the aquarium for heating, lighting, aeration and filtration and it is best to conceal these unnatural items from view as best as one can. External equipment can be placed behind the tank, the back of which is covered with a piece of paper or board. Large photographs of underwater scenes can be purchased which will blend with the contents of the tank. Alternatively, the back of the tank glass can be painted with emulsion in various subtle shades of green, blue or brown. Lighting equipment, in the form of fluorescent tubes, tungsten bulbs or a combination of both, is concealed in the tank cover and care should be taken to ensure that the water level is kept topped up above the line of the top frame, otherwise you will see the glare of the lights directly through the glass.

Heaters, filters and similar within the tank should be concealed behind the rocks or plants. Cables and airtubes should preferably be green in color to disguise them amongst the plants and blend them into the general scene.

43

The aquarist can achieve considerable effect by the careful use of rock and light as is evidenced by this tank designed to display Cichlids.

Undergravel filters are not recommended for use in planted aquaria as they tend to interfere with the healthy development of root systems. Although a correctly balanced tank should not require mechanical filtration, a small airlift filter concealed in a corner will ensure that extra crystal clarity in the water.

Decoration Materials

Rocks and pebbles are widely used in aquaria to provide extra interest. A certain amount of care is necessary in selecting these materials, which could contain mineral salts harmful to the fish and plant occupants of the tank. Limestone should be avoided where the conditions are meant to be acid as the calcium compounds within the rock will soon neutralise the acid content and even turn it alkaline. Neutral rocks such as sandstone, flint, slate or granite are probably the best.

You have a choice of using freshly split, jagged rocks, or weathered rocks and large pebbles with smooth edges. A good source for the latter is the sea-shore or the beds of fast running streams, where unusual shapes are easy to find. All

44

rocks should be thoroughly scrubbed and sterilized with boiling water before being introduced to the aquarium, so that any potential animal or plant parasites are detroyed. Try to use either jagged or weathered rocks, as a mixture of the two usually destroys the aesthetic appeal to the scene. Rocks can be arranged in such a way as to provide terraces and valleys in the landscape, usually with the smaller ones at the front, graduating to larger ones at the rear.

Rocks can be purchased from your supplier but are usually expensive and it is much more fun to search for your own free supply. Artificial rocks, made from concrete or other materials, can also be purchased or you can make your own. The advantage of this is that you can construct rocks to your own specifications. Complete, natural looking 'cliff faces' can be made to retain your terraces. The best materials for constructing rocks are cement, sand and peat mixed together in equal quantities by volume. If you can obtain red sand, the final color of the rocks will be more attractive. Thoroughly mix the dry ingredients together and add water, a little at a time, until you have a workable

An attractive scene can be created at very little cost. Here rock and driftwood are complimented by *Cambomba* and *Bacopa*, whilst colored paper is used as a backdrop to the tank.

Aquariums in zoos are designed by experts to both display the fish and to create natural aquascenes. You can gain from such professional knowledges simply by studying the tanks for ideas.

Rock and driftwood are a feature of the above tank and provide space and shaded areas for the fish. Rock does not have to be especially conspicuous to be an integral part of the scene — as shown below.

mass which can be sculpted to whatever shape you require. With the skilful use of a small trowel or knife and a dry paintbrush, you can make arches, strata, hollows for plants and caves for the fishes to hide in. Although the peat will help neutralize the alkaline content of the cement, after the rocks have thoroughly dried out and solidified, they should be left under running water for a few days to remove all traces of soluble salts. Only when a pH test of the water used to soak the rock reads neutral, should your artificial rocks be used.

Another popular decorative addition to the aquarium is driftwood or bogwood. The former may be part of the branch or the roots of a tree which has been swept out to sea during floods and thoroughly weathered by the action of tide and sand on the sea-shore. This process will abrase it free of bark and the sun will bleach it. Bogwood is usually dredged from the mud in a bog or marsh and may have been there for many years. The lack of oxygen in the mud has a sort of pickling effect on the wood and prevents it from rotting. Attractive pieces of bogwood are often available from your supplier. Driftwood or bogwood should be thoroughly washed and scrubbed in hot water and it is also adviseable to leave it to soak in neutral water for a few days and then checking the pH and hardness before using it in the aquarium. Pieces of wood from living trees should never be used in the aquarium as the sap can be dangerous to both fishes and plants.

The Amazon Sword plant provides the focal point of this tank. The driftwood and attention to illumination complete the scene. Note also the way in which the gravel is sloped to good effect.

Granite, rock, bogwood, artificial and natural plants are used in this tank — all are 'set off' by the careful use of light.

Artificial Plants

The aquarium 'purist' often despises the use of artificial plants but it is a fact that many people today find them very useful and they do have obvious benefits where plant-eating fish are concerned. There are now many kinds of artificial plants available, made from plastic or other inert material. Some of these are so well made that it can be difficult to distinguish them from the real thing. Used sparingly, they can be worked into the underwater environment with the rocks, driftwood and natural plants.

Planting Layout

When planning an aquascene, it is worth remembering to avoid even numbers. Plant one, three or five plants — aesthetically, two of anything is considered a bad combination. Likewise, it is adviseable to arrange the plants so that smaller specimens are in the front, increasing in size as one moves towards the rear of the tank where they may be more densely placed. This not only looks attractive, but is welcomed by the fish for the extra privacy afforded at the back of the tank. One should avoid overplanting to the point where there is no free-swimming area for the fish, and the front of the tank is usually the best place for this. Always plant tall growing, marsh species on terraces at the rear of the tank and other individual species should be placed in small groups separated from each other by rocks or driftwood. Never try and get too many species of plant into one aquarium; it is better to have two or three healthy species than a large number all competing against each other for light and nutrients.

Novelty Tanks

Novelty tanks are increasing in popularity and there is usually a class for these in the larger aquatic shows, particularly in the United States. They are a form of aquascaping that can be made into any theme and usually entail the addition of various 'unnatural' artifacts to the scene. Popular themes are Angels in Heaven, various fictional scenes such as Snow White, Aladdin's Cave, Alice in Wonderland, Sunken Cities, Noah's Ark and that all time favourite Sunken Galleons and Treasure.

Most suppliers stock a range of figures and, of course, the imaginative aquarist will no doubt think of many items which can be used for this purpose to good visual effect. Many aquarists who keep tropical fish, try to build a theme around particular varieties, such as Siamese Fighters, Gouramis, Tiger Barbs, Pirahnas and such. Clearly, goldfish keepers will be in some way influenced by the Chinese-Japanese background of their fish, which leads to all manner of possibilities. It is worth remembering that novelty tanks not only encompass the inside of the tank but also the outside. A little thought to the tank's immediate surroundings can pay handsome dividends.

The display in this picture is an example of how the exterior of a tank can be ornamented — in this case to become a shop window.

Glossary of Terminology

Aerenchyma: A form of plant tissue with numerous air spaces between the cells; found mainly in aquatic plants to which it gives buoyancy.

Annual: A plant which completes its life cycle in one season.

Aquaculture: The science of cultivation of aquatic plants.

Binomial system: The use of generic and specific scientific names in the classification of plants (and animals) devised by Carl Linnaeus.

Chemical prostration: A build up of chemical content to a dangerous level due to the continual topping up of an aquarium with hard water.

Chlorophyll: The green pigment of plants which absorbs light and assists in photosynthesis.

Chloroplast: Small bodies within the cytoplasm of green plant cells, which hold the chlorophyll and assist in the process of photosynthesis.

Diaphototrophic: Describing the situation in which parts of green plants grow horizontally to the light source.

Ecology: The study of living organisms in relation to each other and the environment.

Endodermis: An inner layer of living cells usually surrounding the vascular tissue of plants.

Epidermis: The outer layer of cells in plants.

Heterophylly: The state of bearing leaves of more than one shape or function on the same plant.

Hydrometer: A floating instrument for measuring the specific gravity of fluids.

Lanceolate: Lance-shaped, as usually applied to foliage leaves.

Mesophyll: The green tissue between the epidermal layers of a leaf.

Offset: A shoot which grows from the base of some plants and readily forms a new plant.

Opposed: Paired leaves which grow on opposite sides of the stem.

Perennial: A plant which lives three or more seasons.

Photoperiod: The length of daylight to which many organisms respond.

51

Photosynthesis: The formation of organic substances from water and carbon dioxide via chlorophyll and the energy of sunlight.

Phototropic: The state in which the stems of plants grow towards light (positively phototropic), or away from light (negatively phototropic).

Physiology: The study of the internal functions of plants (and animals).

Reproduction: The act of producing more individuals of the same species.

Rhizome: Horizontal growing stem under or partly underground which may be slender and quick-growing or fleshy and acting as a storage organ.

Rosette: A rose-shaped collection of leaves on a very short stem.

Runner: Stem running along the ground horizontally and forming new plants at the leaf nodes.

Spadix: A flower consisting of a thick fleshy spike surrounded by a spathe.

Spathe: A bract or leaf surrounding a spadix.

Stolon: An aerial (or aquatic) shoot that bends to the substrate and roots at its tip, forming a new plant.

Taxonomy: The science of classification of plants (and animals).

Tuber: Underground storage organ consisting of swollen stems or roots.

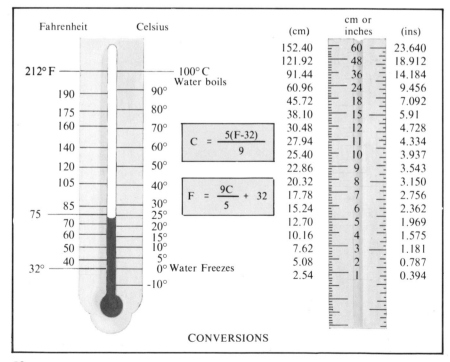

CONVERSIONS